D0999899

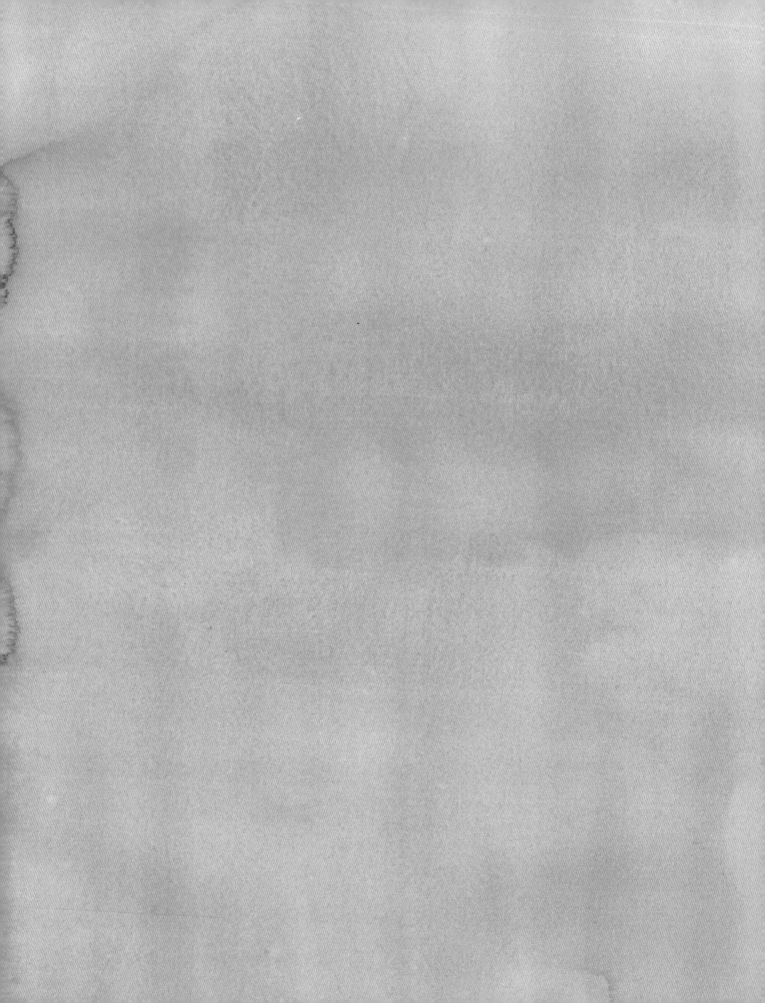

OUT of the WOODS

A True Story of an Unforgettable Event

Rebecca Bond

MARGARET FERGUSON BOOKS
Farrar Straus Giroux
New York

Antonio Willie Giroux lived in Ontario, Canada, in the town of Gowganda, on the edge of Gowganda Lake, in a hotel his mother ran. It was not a fancy place in 1914, but it was big—three stories tall.

There weren't many children to play with, so Antonio
made friends with the hotel workers.

He knew the daily routines of the cooks,   the maids,

and the hired men who stoked the stoves   and maintained the building.

The ground floor of the hotel had a large open space for eating, with the kitchen at one end.

Antonio slept in a room off the kitchen
that had once been a pantry.

The second floor had rooms for travelers passing through
and outdoor sportsmen who would stay for a few days to fish or hunt.
Antonio liked to peek into these rooms when the doors were open.
Even though they had warm, dry beds and woolen blankets like his own,
these rooms were much more interesting. They also had the guests' canvas
travel bags with many pockets, nets and poles for fishing, and sometimes
even guns.

But the top floor was Antonio's favorite—one great room lined
with rows of bunk beds. It was here where the men who worked in the
forest—trappers, lumberjacks, and silver miners—lived for months at a
time. Here it smelled wonderful—of sweet tobacco and wood, wool and
leather, and sweat. Here Antonio could listen to French and English
and Native American languages, sometimes all spoken at once.

And up here in the evenings the men played cards and made music, told boisterous stories and laughed. Antonio loved how the top floor of the hotel was very noisy until the lanterns were blown out and everyone fell asleep. Only then did it become so quiet that he could hear the fir boughs brushing against the windowpanes.

Surrounding the hotel was a dense forest, mostly cedar, pine, balsam, and poplar trees. When Antonio walked through the forest, he heard the bay of wolves getting ready to chase deer, saw the tracks of foxes hunting mice, and noticed the signs of bear, moose, and weasel: fur rubbed off on bark, a sleeping impression in the earth, a hollow log lined with dry grass.

These half glimpses were never enough for Antonio. But
he also knew that in Gowganda, with its trappers, hunters,
and lumberjacks who made tall trees crash to the ground,
the safest place for the animals was a distant, hidden one.

When Antonio was almost five, the summer was so dry the
green carpets of moss yellowed, the silky grass crisped, and the
pine needles on the trees turned brittle. One day, a miner on the
third floor spotted smoke in the hills and sounded the alarm.
Antonio knew they were all in real danger.

The news spread fast; the fire spread faster.
Antonio watched as the wind pushed the fire in
every direction. He heard it roar like a monster
and crackle with white lightning heat. Soon
there was only one place to go.

All the people of Gowganda—hotel guests, trappers, lumberjacks, silver miners, cooks, maids, hired men, Antonio's mother, and Antonio—went into the lake. There was even a baby, not half a year old, held in his mother's arms. They stood in the water up to their knees, their waists, their shoulders and stared as the fire came closer and closer.

And then through the smoke
and flames Antonio saw something
remarkable. Out of the forest and
into the lake came foxes and rabbits,
bobcats and raccoons.

Wolves appeared, and deer, and moose.
Porcupines and elk. Squirrels and possums.
Even some bears.
Antonio watched as all the animals came
out of the thickets and down from treetops
and stood in Gowganda Lake as the forest
around them burned.

Wolves stood beside deer, foxes beside rabbits.
And people and moose stood close enough to touch.

Antonio smelled the steam rising off the animals' wet fur, saw their chests lifting and falling in steady rhythm, and felt their hot animal breath.

Antonio didn't know how long everyone stood there, but it
felt like several days. The fierce fire and smoke made the sky so
black no one could tell whether it was day or night.

Finally, the monster stopped roaring. The red flames blew themselves out. The black sky turned charcoal gray, heather gray, and then almost blue. It was safe, at last, to leave the lake.

Miraculously, the hotel had not burned down.

Antonio went back to sleeping in the room next to the kitchen.

Hotel guests still had rooms on the second floor with warm, dry beds and woolen blankets.

The trappers and lumberjacks and miners returned to their bunks on the third floor.

Antonio continued to live in Gowganda for the
next ten years of his life.

He stayed friends with the cooks, the maids, and
the hired men. He listened to the stories told by the
lumberjacks, and sometimes he went fishing with
the fishermen.

He swam in the cold lake.

But Antonio never forgot the fire or the people up to their waists in water.

Mostly, he never forgot how he had watched that distance between animals and people disappear in the summer of 1914, when he was almost five years old.

Antonio Willie Giroux

AUTHOR'S NOTE

This is a true story. Antonio Willie Giroux was my grandfather. He lived in the Gowganda Hotel until he was fourteen years old, when he moved to the United States and learned to speak English (he had spoken only French until then).

I know many stories about my grandfather—about the farm he had for many years, about the carpentry work he did all over the state of Vermont, even about his joyful reunion with Native American half siblings—brothers and sisters he learned about only when he was an old man.

But it is this story of Papa that is my favorite. He told it to his children, and my mother told it to me.

Though my children will never know Antonio Willie Giroux, I will tell them this story of their great-grandfather and that remarkable thing that happened to him when he was a boy in Gowganda, Ontario.